SUPER SIMPLE

# KITCHEN GARDENS

## A KID'S GUIDE TO GARDENING

ALEX KUSKOWSKI

Consulting Editor, Diane Craig, M.A./Reading Specialist

Super Sandcastle

An Imprint of Abdo Publishing
www.abdopublishing.com

SUPER SIMPLE GARDENING

**www.abdopublishing.com**

Published by Abdo Publishing, a division of ABDO, PO Box 398166, Minneapolis, Minnesota 55439. 

Printed in the United States of America, North Mankato, Minnesota
102014
012015

THIS BOOK CONTAINS RECYCLED MATERIALS

Editor: Liz Salzmann
Content Developer: Alex Kuskowski
Cover and Interior Design and Production: Mighty Media, Inc.
Photo Credits: Jen Schoeller, Shutterstock

**Library of Congress Cataloging-in-Publication Data**

Kuskowski, Alex.
Super simple kitchen gardens : a kid's guide to gardening / Alex Kuskowski.
pages cm. -- (Super simple gardening)
ISBN 978-1-62403-525-8
1. Kitchen gardens--Juvenile literature. 2. Vegetable gardening--Juvenile literature. I. Title. II. Series: Kuskowski, Alex. Super simple gardening.
SB324.K87 2015
635--dc23
2014023976

Super SandCastle™ books are created by a team of professional educators, reading specialists, and content developers around five essential components—phonemic awareness, phonics, vocabulary, text comprehension, and fluency—to assist young readers as they develop reading skills and strategies and increase their general knowledge. All books are written, reviewed, and leveled for guided reading, early reading intervention, and Accelerated Reader® programs for use in shared, guided, and independent reading and writing activities to support a balanced approach to literacy instruction.

# TO ADULT HELPERS

Gardening is a lifelong skill. It is fun and simple to learn. There are a few things to remember to keep kids safe. Gardening requires commitment. Help your children stay dedicated to watering and caring for their plants. Some activities in this book recommend adult supervision. Some use sharp tools. Be sure to review the activities before starting and be ready to assist your budding gardeners when necessary.

## Key Symbol

In this book you may see this symbol. Here is what it means.

**Inside Light**
Put your plant inside.
**Direct Light** = in sunlight.
**Indirect Light** = in shade.

# TABLE OF CONTENTS

# GET INTO GARDENING

Grow a garden you can use! Start planning your kitchen garden. Plant **herbs** you can cook with. Grow plants that will make your kitchen smell good.

It is easy to start. This book will give you simple tips. Explore the world of gardening. Get your hands dirty. Grow something great!

# KITCHEN GARDENS

A kitchen garden is a garden that you grow indoors. It has edible or sweet-smelling plants. Choose a few **herbs** to add to your kitchen garden:

### Edible Herbs

Basil, chives, cilantro, dill, mint, oregano, parsley, rosemary, thyme

### Sweet-Smelling

Lavender, eucalyptus, vanilla butterfly plant

# PLANT PLANNING

Kitchen gardens take careful planning. Learn about the plants you choose for your garden. Find out what they need to be healthy.

## Inside Gardens

Indoor plants need a safe place. Follow these rules to choose the best area in your home!

- Make sure they won't get knocked over or stepped on.
- Put them where the temperature stays about the same.
- Make sure the plants get sunlight. Put them near a window.

## Plant Tip

Set a watering **schedule**. Check the soil to see if your plants need water. Stick a finger into the soil ½ inch (1.3 cm). If it is dry, the plant may need water.

# TOOLS

These are some of the important gardening tools you will be using for the projects in this book.

containers & pots

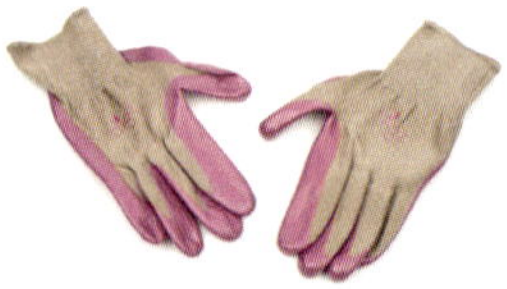

garden gloves

hand trowel

plants

soil

rocks

watering can

scissors

# SAFETY

Be safe and responsible while gardening. There are a few rules for doing gardening projects.

### Ask Permission

Get **permission** to do a project. You might want to use tools or things around the house. Ask first!

### Be Safe

Get help from an adult when using sharp tools or moving something heavy.

### Clean Up

Clean up your working area when you are finished. Put everything away.

# DIG INTO DIRT

Soil is more than just dirt. It is the key to gardening. Help your kitchen garden grow with the right soil.

Choose the best soil for your plants. If you don't know, ask a gardener for help.

### Desert Potting Mix

This soil works best with **cacti** and other **succulents**.

### All-Purpose Potting Mix

This soil works well with most plants in pots. Buy soil with **peat moss** and **vermiculite**.

# STARTING FROM SEED

- Read the package the seeds came in. It will say how much water and sunlight the seeds need.
- Fill a biodegradable **container** with soil. See page 16 to learn how to make your own biodegradable containers.
- Pack down the soil with your hands. Add water to the soil.
- Place a seed in the soil. Cover it up. Follow the instructions on the package.
- Watch for your plant to sprout. Then you can plant it in a bigger pot.

# MOVING ON UP!

After your seed sprouts, it needs more space. Its roots need room to grow. Here's how to replant your seedling.

- Water the seedling 1 hour before replanting it.
- Fill a pot with soil. Dig a hole in the soil.
- Place the biodegradable **container** in the hole. Cover it with soil. Make sure the seedling sticks out of the soil.
- Water the plant.

### Use the Right Size Pot

Plants need room to grow! The roots should not touch the sides of the pot.

**TIP**

Some pots have holes in the bottom. This helps drain extra water. They should be placed on **saucers** to catch the water.

### Small Pots

Pots less than 8 inches (20 cm) deep.

### Medium Pots

Pots 8 inches (20 cm) to 16 inches (40.5 cm) deep.

### Large Pots

Pots deeper than 16 inches (40.5 cm).

# COOL CARE

### Rocks

Some pots need rocks in the bottom. This helps the water drain out of the soil. It keeps the roots from getting too wet.

### The Right Light

Light is important! Get the right light for your plants. Check how many hours of sunlight your plants need.

To get the right light, know what direction the windows face. South facing windows give the most light. East and west facing windows have a medium amount of light. North facing windows have the least light.

# USE IT!

Kitchen gardens are useful. Use the **herbs** you grow to give your meals a new flavor. Use other plants you grow to give your house a sweet smell. Here are some ideas to get started.

- Top pastas with fresh rosemary and basil.
- Cut up a few chives for your morning eggs.
- Chop up some cilantro to use in your next batch of salsa.
- Cut sprigs of lavender. Dry it and hang the sweet-smelling herb in your room.

# HERB PLANTER

START YOUR SEEDS IN THESE!

## Supplies

green paper
scissors (optional)
measuring cup
blender
spoon
rag
muffin tin
paper towels
potting soil
garden gloves
cilantro seeds
fertilizer

# DIRECTIONS

1. Cut or tear the paper into small pieces. Make 4 cups of paper pieces.
2. Put the paper pieces in the blender. Add 3¼ cups water.
3. Blend 30 seconds. Stop the blender. Use a spoon to push the paper down. Blend for 1 minute. Stir again. Keep blending and stirring for 5 minutes.
4. Pour the paper **pulp** onto the rag. Squeeze out the extra water.

Project continues on the next page

1

2

4

5 Put a handful of **pulp** in a muffin cup.

6 Press the pulp into an even layer on the bottom.

7 Add pulp to the sides. Make all the pulp an even thickness.

8 Press a paper towel in the cup to remove any water. Put pulp in the other cups the same way. Let the pulp dry 48 hours.

9 Take the paper cups out of the tin. Put potting soil in each cup.

10 Put three seeds in the middle of the cup. Cover with a thin layer of soil. Water the seeds.

11 Put the cups in a sunny spot. Water them when the soil feels dry. Add **fertilizer** once a month.

**COOL CARE**

When the seedlings get bigger, plant them outside. Plant them in the paper cups. The cups will **decompose**.

# PIZZA GARDEN

GROW THE HERBS USED TO MAKE PIZZA!

INSIDE
DIRECT SUN

## Supplies

- 3 small plant containers
- painter's tape
- chalkboard paint
- foam brush
- potting soil
- garden gloves
- hand trowel
- 1 basil seedling
- 1 thyme seedling
- 1 oregano seedling
- chalk
- fertilizer

# DIRECTIONS

1. Tape off a square area on the side of each **container**.
2. Paint inside the taped square with chalkboard paint. Let the paint dry.
3. Fill each pot about halfway with potting soil.

**Project continues on the next page**

1

2

3

4 Make a hole in the dirt of each **container**.

5 Take the basil seedling out of its tray. Pull gently at the roots to loosen them.

6 Put the seedling in a container. Fill in the container with dirt.

7 Take the thyme seedling out of its tray. Pull gently at the roots to loosen them. Put the seedling in the second container. Fill in the container with dirt.

8 Plant the oregano seedling in the third **container**. Water each plant.

9 Use chalk to write the plant names on the containers.

10 Put the plants in a spot that gets sun 5 hours a day. Water the soil when it feels dry. Add **fertilizer** once a month.

8

9

10

**COOL CARE**

You can harvest the leaves of **herb** plants after a few weeks. Take only a few leaves at a time.

# SWEET SMELLS

GROW A PLANT THAT SMELLS GREAT!

INSIDE
DIRECT SUN

## Supplies

2-liter bottle

ruler

marker

scissors

duct tape

cotton fabric, 8 inches (20 cm) square

garden gloves

hand trowel

vanilla butterfly seedling

watering can

# DIRECTIONS

1. Measure 5 inches (12.7 cm) from the bottom of the bottle. Draw a line around the bottle.

2. Have an adult help you cut along the line.

3. Cover the outside of the bottle halves with duct tape. Use colorful duct tape for decoration!

Project continues on the next page

1

2

3

4. Tie a knot in one corner of the fabric.

5. Put the fabric inside the top half of the bottle. Pull the fabric through the opening. Pull until the knot catches.

6. Put the top half of the bottle in the bottom half.

7. Fill the bottle halfway with soil. Take the seedling out of its tray. Put the seedling in the bottle.

8 Add soil to fill the bottle. Press down gently. Make sure the seedling is firmly in place.

9 Lift the top half of the bottle out. Fill the bottom half one-third full of water.

10 Put the top of the bottle back in the bottom. Water the seedling.

11 Place the seedling in a sunny spot. Add water to the bottom half of the bottle every 3 to 4 days.

**COOL TIP**

Put the duct tape on in small pieces. It will stick better!

8

9

10

# HERB SAVER

DRY YOUR HERBS TO USE LATER!

## Supplies

newspaper
large wooden picture frame
acrylic paint
foam brush
4 large wooden beads
heavy-duty glue
cotton fabric
scissors
stapler
small glass squares
paper towels
whiteboard marker
jars
labels

# DIRECTIONS

1. Cover your work area with newspaper. Take the glass and backing out of the frame.

2. Paint the picture frame. Let the paint dry.

3. Paint the beads to match the picture frame. Let the paint dry.

4. Turn the picture frame over. Glue a bead to each corner of the frame.

Project continues on the next page

**5** Cut the fabric so it's slightly larger than the frame opening.

**6** Have an adult help staple the fabric to the back of the frame. Start by stapling the corners. Make sure the fabric is tight across the frame.

**7** Staple the sides of the fabric to the frame. Use two to three staples per side.

**8** Glue three glass squares to one side of the frame. Space them evenly. Let the glue dry.

# DRYING HERBS

1. Watch for plant buds. It is best to pick **herbs** after plant buds form. Use scissors to cut off a branch.

2. Gently pull off the leaves. Wash them carefully. Pat them dry.

3. Place the leaves on the fabric. Don't let them overlap. Write the herb names on the glass squares with a whiteboard marker.

4. Put the frame in a safe space. Check the leaves in 1 to 2 weeks. If they **crumble**, put them in a jar. Label the jar with the herb name and the date. Herbs last 1 year.

1

2

3

# GLOSSARY

**cactus** – a plant with sharp spikes instead of leaves that grows in hot dry places.

**container** – something that other things can be put into.

**crumble** – to break into small pieces.

**decompose** – to break down or rot.

**fertilizer** – something used to make plants grow better in soil.

**herb** – a scented plant used to flavor food or make medicine.

**peat moss** – a type of moss that usually grows on wet land and is used in gardening.

**permission** – when a person in charge says it's okay to do something.

**pulp** – a soft, wet mixture made with wood, paper, or fabric.

**saucer** – a shallow dish that goes under something to catch spills.

**schedule** – a list of the times when things will happen.

**succulent** – a plant, such as a cactus or an aloe, that has thick stems or leaves that store water.

**vermiculite** – a light material that holds water that is often added to potting soil.